Also by
Lynn Schmalz

What Is School?

Order copies at
www.amazon.com
www.barnesandnoble.com

Autographed copies available
via email at
lynnschmalz@sbcglobal.net

What Is Church?

By Lynn Schmalz

A Pedal Down Promotions

Publication

Manitowoc, Wisconsin

What Is Church?

By Lynn Schmalz

Front and back cover design: Kathy Roehrig, Pedal Down Promotions

Front cover, back cover and interior illustrations: Lynn Schmalz

ISBN- 979-8-435-41758-6

Published by Pedal Down Promotions
Manitowoc, Wisconsin
www.pedaldownpromo.com
pedaldownpromotions@gmail.com
920-323-7970

I would like to thank God from whom all blessings flow; especially Talya Ray Kruse and Retta Grace Kruse, Anita, Todd, Amanda Kruse, Andy, Douglas and James H. Schmalz, Ruth C. Banaszynski, Ian, Tabitha and Nicole.

Karen Lueders, who wrote "To God Be The Glory" encouraged me to write my books.
Thank you Karen!

Pastor Andrew T. Luehring reviewed my book and gave positive feedback. I thank him for making time to do so and for being a blessing in the lives of so many through his faithful teaching and preaching of the Truth...God's Word is Truth, amen!

What is the church but a gathering place for every soul, regardless of race?

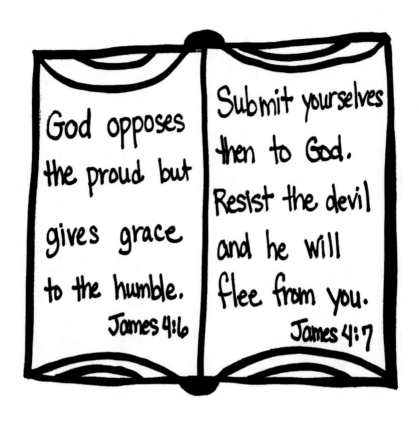

God opposes the proud but gives grace to the humble.
James 4:6

Submit yourselves then to God. Resist the devil and he will flee from you.
James 4:7

For we all were created by the Creator, who gave us the Bible...or we wouldn't have a clue.

For in the beginning,
Adam and Eve, to their God,
they did cleave.
Yet the devil was jealous and
lied to the two.
They fell for the lie and sin
came through.

Adam and Eve were stuck in
their sin and banned from
paradise.
They were separated from
God...that was the price.

Why did they stumble?
They lost their goal.
They were not humble.
They sold their soul.

Me, me, me...
I want...
They were selfish!
I'm #1.
Not God's will, but what I
wish, that's what I want.
That's more fun!

God's will	My will
Love God above all	I'm the boss
Love one another	I want things my way
God is invisible, immortal, all knowing, all powerful and everywhere	I know better

Sin is doing evil, not what is right.

It lives in darkness and avoids the light.

The devil wants to be worshipped; he wants the praise.

He will tempt us to sin all of his days.

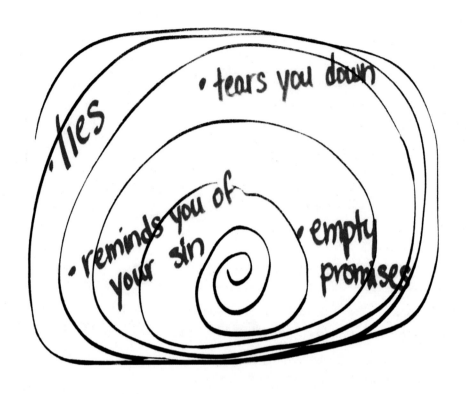

The devil is tricky.
He was a greedy angel
that fell.
He makes life sticky, wishing
all to go to hell.

Yet in our baptism, through water and God's word, the truth of Jesus' life is what we have heard.

Jesus came to Earth from
Heaven above.
He is God and man, who
shows us his love.
He lived to obey God and
died innocently.
What an awesome
sacrifice for you and me.

He is the shepherd and we are
the sheep.
We need him all of our days.
Why he loves us, I don't know,
yet his promises he does keep.
Yet we are forgetful in so
many ways.

God is mysterious, majestic
and perfect, you see.
His creation is not...Oh boy!
Pity me!
We are lost without God; we
are hopeless, it's true!
What in the world can we
do?

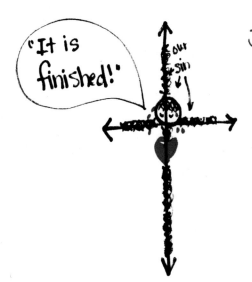

We can do nothing...Oh, how grim.

We can not...but leave it to him!

God sent his son Jesus to take our place.

All of our sins on Him...what grace!

(undeserved love)

Jesus rose,
beating death altogether.
Faith is a gift,
Jesus is the treasure!

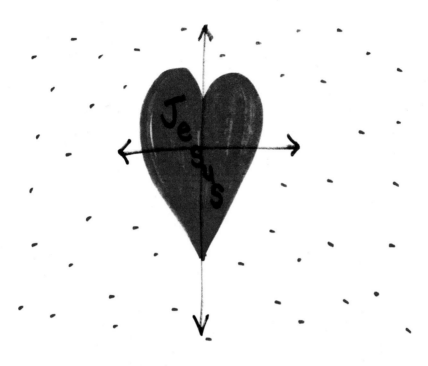

For we know that God loves
us...what more could he do?
He gave all he had to save me
and you!

In God I trust; I will not be afraid.

Love God above all... Thy will be done!

I am sorry for sinning against you God. Please, help me to learn from my mistakes and do better for your glory, Amen.

Thank you God for loving me.

The church is the people who trust and obey... the Bible; Jesus' teachings to repent, listen and pray.

'We love' because, He' loved
, us first!

We are not perfect, yet
together we love.
Not of ourselves...it's a gift
from above.

So, the church is all believers, and Jesus is the head.
He's the way, truth and life...without him we are dead!

My cup overflows · Psalm 23

We can love because he loved
us first.
His word gives us life giving
water...no more thirst!

There's a purpose and a plan
for all, you see.
Encourage and love all, shine
his light and be the hands
and feet of Jesus to all in
your sphere.
Where two or three are
gathered, Jesus draws near.

With God all things are
possible, this is true!
Let's thank God every day
for giving us life anew!

Jesus opened the gate
between God and us.
He is the way; in him we
trust.

So come to the building to hear God's word, then go share his love until all have heard.
We are the church, so now that you know...be his light...reflect Jesus wherever you go!

So let's learn more of Jesus
all of our days.
To the only true God give
thanks and eternal praise!
Amen!

About the Author

I am Lynn Schmalz. I enjoy being a paraprofessional for the Kimberly Area School District.

I am married to Douglas Schmalz for 30 years and counting. We have a daughter Amanda (Schmalz) Kruse, son-in-law Todd Kruse, granddaughters Talya Ray Kruse and Retta Grace Kruse and a son Andrew Schmalz.

I grew up in Kaukauna, Wisconsin with a younger sister Kristy, and a younger brother Michael. Our Mom, Ruth (Raaths) Banaszynski was our first teacher. She instilled in me an unquenchable love of learning!

I am still learning from her and others...thanks Mom!

I love being involved in mission work, including Central African Medical Mission, Lutheran Women's Mission Society, Sunday School, the Hope Center/Pillars and playing organ. I believe Jesus died for me, so I believe I will live for him.

I wrote and illustrated my first children's book "What Is School?" in 2021. "What Is Church?" is my second children's book.

"Whatsoever you do to the least of our brothers that you do unto me," Jesus said.

To God be glory, because of Jesus through the Holy Spirit, hallelujah and Amen!